T0284065

401(k) Plans Made Easy

Understanding your 401(k) Plan

Suzan M. Hall, CFS®

Important Disclaimers

ISBN: 979-8-35094-801-1 (print)
ISBN: 979-8-35094-229-3 (eBook)

Table of Contents

Chapter 1

What is a 401(k) Plan?

Introduction and history of 401(k) retirement plans and why you should start saving now

What exactly is a 401(k) plan?

I am so glad you asked. Let's start with the basics. A 401(k) is a section of the Internal Revenue Code, 40l(k). It is an employer-sponsored retirement plan that typically allows employees to contribute to the plan directly from each paycheck via payroll deduction. It allows employees to save for retirement during their working years, so they can retire with dignity when the time comes.

Depending on the plan design, employees can usually contribute on a pre-tax basis and Roth 401(k) "post-tax" basis. More on that later. Roth 401(k) contributions are becoming the golden standard within 401(k)s, so if you don't see this option in your plan, it may be time for the employer to reevaluate the current plan document.

Because a 401(k) is an employer-sponsored retirement plan, employees are not able to set up their own 401(k) at their local bank or through their advisor. You must own a business in order to establish a 401(k) plan for a company. Employees of a company offering a 401(k) plan can contribute via salary deferrals directly from their paycheck each pay period. A 401(k) is often viewed as a retirement plan benefit or perk for working at an organization.

Most 401(k) plans are considered participant-directed, which means the employee (participant) gets to choose from a menu of investment options that are usually made up of mutual funds, CITs, Target Date Funds or a mix of all of these. Some plans may also offer a self-directed brokerage account to allow employees to link their 401(k) to a brokerage account so they can invest in individual stocks, bonds, ETFs, mutual funds, and more complex investment vehicles.

History of 401(k) Plans

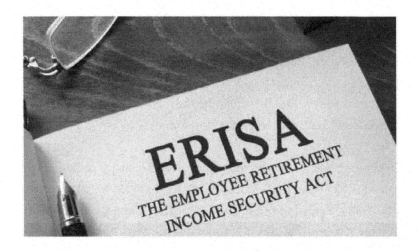

On November 6,1978, President Jimmy Carter signed the Revenue Act and the Internal Revenue Service Tax Code, 401(k), was born. It allowed employers to offer a retirement plan where employees could defer their own compensation on a tax-deferred basis into a 401(k) plan. This new method of pre-tax savings was designed to prevent profit sharing plans from only benefiting top executives.

A 401(k) plan became governed by ERISA, the Employee Retirement Income Securities Act to ensure non-discrimination between highly compensated and key employees compared to the non-highly compensated, rank-and-file employees.

Traditional pension plans that promised a certain monthly benefit to employees at retirement were becoming too expensive to maintain as they were 100% employer funded, so more and more businesses began freezing their pension plans and added a 401(k) plan to relieve some of the financial burden and create generous tax benefits to business owners and their employees. Over the next 43 years, numerous legislative rulings paved the trail for the 401(k) plans we see today.

4

As you can see in the historical contribution chart, 401(k) contribution limits have increased tremendously over the years, even into 2024. Salary deferrals can be pre-tax and Roth up to the salary deferral limit while the Catch-Up contribution is currently pre-tax only as of the writing of this book. Catch-up contributions allow an employee an additional contribution over the salary deferral limit. A participant who is age 50 or older by the end of 2023 can contribute up to $30,000.

Historical 401(k) Salary Deferral IRS Contribution Limits
1997-2024

YEAR	SALARY DEFERRAL LIMIT	AGE 50+ CATCH-UP LIMIT
2024	$23,000	$7,500
2023	$22,500	$7,500
2022	$20,500	$6,500
2021	$19,500	$6,500
2020	$19,500	$6,500
2019	$19,000	$6,000
2018	$18,500	$6,000
2017	$18,000	$6,000
2016	$18,000	$6,000
2015	$18,000	$6,000
2014	$17,500	$5,500
2013	$17,500	$5,500
2012	$17,000	$5,500
2011	$16,500	$5,500
2010	$16,500	$5,500
2009	$16,500	$5,500
2008	$15,500	$5,000
2007	$15,500	$5,000
2006	$15,000	$5,000
2005	$14,000	$4,000
2004	$13,000	$3,000
2003	$12,000	$2,000
2002	$11,000	$1,000
2001	$10,500	
2000	$10,500	
1999	$10,000	
1998	$10,000	
1997	$9,500	

Today, people are living longer and your "pot of gold" for retirement is like a three-legged stool. Your retirement income will likely come from three main sources. Social security benefits, savings, IRA or pension (if you're lucky to get a pension), and your 401(k). The majority of your income in retirement will come from your own 401(k) if you start saving early during your working years. It is a lot harder to save when you're not making money if you wait until retirement to start saving!

Social security benefits were never meant to be a primary source of income in retirement and there has been much debate on the political landscape over the past twenty plus years as to whether or not they will even be available when you reach retirement age. You can check out your own estimated monthly social security benefits by going to www.ssn.gov to download a current statement based on your work history. Not all jobs pay into social security, however. For example, police officers and firefighters usually have their own pension plan, so they would not pay into the social security system.

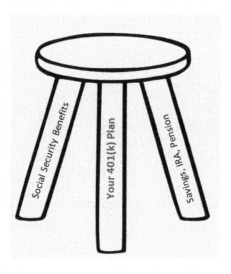

Why Save in a 401(k) versus a Regular Savings Account?

One of the biggest benefits of saving in a 401(k) plan compared to a regular savings account is the *tax deferred* benefit. Not only do *contributions* grow tax-free while in the account, but the *earnings* also grow tax-free year after year until you take the money out of the account, which we'll talk about later in this book. A regular savings account is *not* tax deferred. Instead, you pay taxes up front on the amount you place into a savings account and at the end of each year, you pay taxes on any earnings or interest from the savings account unlike a 401(k) plan. Let's check out a hypothetical example:

Assumes $80k annual salary/semi-monthly paycheck/10% contribution		
	Bank Savings Account	**401(k) Account**
Gross pay semi-monthly	$3,333	$3,333
Pre-tax savings	$0	$333
Post-tax savings	$333	**$0**
Taxable income	$3,333	**$3,000**
FICA taxes (8.65%)	$288	$288
Income taxes (24%)	$800	$720
Total take home pay	$1,912	**$1,992**

*This is not tax advice. Please consult with a CPA for specific tax guidance.

That's an additional $80 in your pocket each pay period or $1,920 more per year in your pocket! Saving in a 401(k) results in less taxes being paid and more money in your pocket when compared to saving in a bank account. This of course does not mean you shouldn't save in a bank account. It is still an excellent savings tool for short-term expenses. The cost of waiting could cost you thousands of dollars, so start saving in your 401(k) now! If that doesn't convince you, let's look at how the cost of waiting will impact your account balance over time.

The Cost of Waiting

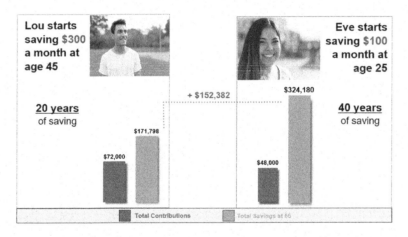

*This scenario assumes a hypothetical 8% annual rate of return for the life of the 401(k)

In this example, we have two 401(k) investors. Eve, the early investor, saves one hundred dollars per month starting at age 25 until she retires at age 65. Lou, the late investor, waits to start saving until he's older and making more money, so beginning at age 45, he saves $300 per month until he is 65. Notice that Eve only had to contribute $48,000 of her own money into the plan with her $100 per month for 40 years, but late Lou contributes $72,000 of his own money into the plan over 20 years. Assuming an 8% annual rate of return in this example, look at the total savings Eve has accumulated while only putting in $48,000. She now has a whopping $324,000! Although Lou put in more of his own money, he lost 20 years to save and have compounding interest working for him, so he only has $171,000 at age 65. Eve ends up with over $152,000 more than Lou. Why is that? It's because she started saving early! Even a small amount each pay period goes a long way the sooner you begin to save.

Chapter 2

Contribution Types

Let's focus on the various types of employee and employer contributions next!

Types of Employee Contributions

The most common types of employee contributions seen in a 401(k) are pre-tax and Roth salary deferrals. Salary deferrals for both pre-tax and Roth 401(k) contributions are deducted directly from an employee's paycheck via payroll deduction.

Pre-tax salary deferrals do not incur state or federal income taxes until a withdrawal is made. That means the employee does not pay state or federal income taxes (ordinary income taxes) on the contributions or on the earnings year after year until the money is cashed out. This is one of the most appealing reasons to contribute to a 401(k) plan - the tax deferral benefits. This concept is called compounding interest, which is interest growing on interest so your account will grow by your contributions and interest earned day after day, creating a snowball effect on your account.

Roth 401(k) salary deferrals are taxed differently than pre-tax salary deferrals. Roth contributions in a 401(k) are first taxed as ordinary income, but the earnings will grow tax-free if certain requirements are met. You still create the snowball effect because compounding interest will occur, and it is tax-free! This can be a good option for employees early in their careers while in a lower tax bracket or for higher earners who do not qualify for the Roth IRA, which has income restrictions.

Note that the Roth IRA is different than the Roth 401(k). Roth contributions in a 401(k) are available to anyone eligible for the 401(k) plan as long as that money source is offered in the plan. The Roth 401(k) has no income restrictions and the limits are much greater than in a Roth IRA.

Unlike the Roth 401(k), a Roth IRA does have income limitations. Depending on multiple factors, such as your tax filing status and your modified adjusted gross income (MAGI), you may not be eligible to make Roth IRA contributions. If you are eligible to make Roth IRA contributions, the limits for 2023 are $6,500 or $7,500 for age 50 and older.

Employees can contribute into both money sources if both are offered in the plan, or they can choose one money source as long as the 402(g) limit is not exceeded in that year. The 402(g) limit is the calendar year salary deferral limit between *all* 401(k) plans you may contribute to.

In 2023, the 402(g) limit was $22,500 for participants under age 50 and $30,000 for those age 50 or older.This limit includes both pre-tax and Roth salary deferrals into a 401(k).For example, you can contribute $10,000 in pre-tax contributions and $12,500 as Roth 401(k) contributions directly from your paycheck for a total of $22,500, meeting the 402(g) limit. If you're age 50 or older in 2023, you can contribute an additional $7,500, called a catch-up contribution, for a total of $30,000.

Keep in mind that if you are contributing to more than one 40l(k), the total employee contribution limit (402(g) limit) is still maxed out at $22,500 for 2023 if you are under age 50. For instance, if you work at company A and company B and they both allow you to contribute to their 40l(k) plan, there is only *one* 402(g) limit between both companies. This is a critical piece of information to know when you have multiple jobs and contribute to each of them.

This rule also applies if you *own* a company and work for someone else and participate in a 40l(k) at both entities. A common question that participants often ask is: do rollovers count towards the 402(g) limit? The answer is no. Rollovers into a 401(k) plan do not count towards the 402(g) limit.

Types of Employer Contributions

Employers are not required to make company contributions, but it is certainly helpful to contribute towards an employee's retirement future to not only show appreciation, but to also use as a company retention tool. If your company offers a match of any kind, the best thing you can do for yourself is to contribute at least up to the maximum matching amount so you don't leave any free money on the table.

Matching contributions are free money! They offer an instant high return on your 401(k) account, often at 25%, 50%, and 100% return! Here are some of the common employer contributions you may see and what they mean:

Discretionary Matching is when a company may or may not make a company match contribution in a given year. It is not required, but the company decides each year. For example, the match may not be written into the plan document, but the company may decide to match 100% up to the first 3% of pay for 2023. Another way to say this, the company match is dollar for dollar up to the first 3% of pay the employee defers into the plan.

Example 1:

Annual Salary: $100,000

Matching Formula: 100% up to the first 5% of pay

Employee Defers $5,000 for the year

Employer Discretionary Match = $5,000

In the above example, you should contribute at least 3% of your pay in order to get the maximum amount of "free money" aka matching dollars from your employer. This would be an instant 100% return on the first 3% of pay that you contribute into the plan, something that most investments alone are unable to offer.

What if we used the same example above except the employee contributes 10% of pay instead of only 5%? Let's take a look:

Example 2:

Annual Salary: $100,000

Matching Formula: 100% up to the first 5% of pay

Employee Defers $10,000 for the year (that's 10% of annual salary)

Employer Discretionary Match = $5,000

The employee will still only receive matching dollars up to 5% of pay, nothing beyond that in this example. Matching dollars and its earnings will remain in your account on a pre-tax basis until you withdrawal the money.

Discretionary Profit Sharing is an optional employer contribution that may be a provision in the plan, but that doesn't mean the company is making that contribution type each year. It is typically not a required contribution by your company. It is up to the employer's discretion as to whether or not the company will offer a profit sharing contribution from year to year. If a company does decide to offer a profit sharing contribution, there are several types of allocation methods used.

It is important to note that if you are eligible for the profit sharing contribution and the employer decides to make the contribution, then it would go to the employee regardless of whether or not he or she participates in the plan, which we'll briefly review in a moment.

The great thing about a profit sharing contribution is that the employee only needs to be *eligible* for the plan in order to receive a profit sharing contribution if the company decides to make one for the year. He or she does not have to *participate* in the plan because it is not the same as a matching contribution. Profit sharing contributions are like a generous pre-tax "bonus" that helps the employee save for retirement. Matching contributions are literally *matching* an employee's salary deferral.

Types of Profit Sharing Allocation Methods

Profit sharing contributions most commonly use one of these allocation methods, which is written into the plan document:

Pro-Rata – This means each eligible employee will either receive the same percentage of pay contribution or the same dollar amount, regardless of your role at the company.

FICA-Integrated – This is similar to Pro-Rata except that employees making over the FICA Social Security Wage Base may be eligible to receive a larger profit sharing contribution.

New Comparability or Cross-Tested – This means that employees are put into participant "groups" and each group may receive a different contribution amount or percentage. This method often favors maximum contributions to owners, key employees and/or executives while giving a minimum contribution to the rest of the employees.

Employer Safe Harbor Contributions

Safe Harbor employer contributions are very common among 401(k) plans. A safe harbor plan can offer retirement plan compliance relief to the plan. This means the company promises to make a "safe harbor" employer contribution to ensure a fail-safe 401(k) plan and automatically pass the standard compliance tests each year.

Safe harbor contributions are mandatory, not discretionary. Please take note of this. The employer is obligated to make an employer safe harbor contribution following the rules of the particular type of safe harbor contribution selected. We'll review shortly. Most safe harbor plans are immediately vested and they can sometimes help Highly Compensated Employees (HCE) and owners to contribute the IRS maximum salary deferrals regardless of what the rest of the Non Highly Compensated Employees (NHCE) are contributing to the plan.

A safe harbor plan can also prevent HCEs and owners from receiving refunds. If you've ever received a refund from your 401(k) contribution, it is most likely because your plan was not a safe harbor and had to undergo annual non-discrimination compliance testing, which failed and required a refund in order to pass the test. Companies can avoid this issue if the plan is set up as a safe harbor.

Types of Employer Safe Harbor Contributions

Basic Safe Harbor Match
- Employer matches 100% up to 3% of pay, then 50% up to the next 2% of pay deferred
- Requires 100% immediate vesting

Enhanced Safe Harbor Match

- Employer matches 100% up to 4% of pay or can be higher
- Requires 100% immediate vesting

Safe Harbor 3% Non-Elective Contribution (NEC)

- Employer makes a non-elective contribution of 3% of pay to all eligible employees regardless of whether or not they participate
- It is not a match, but a non-elective contribution

QACA Safe Harbor (Qualified Automatic Contribution Arrangement)

- Employer matches 100% up to the 1% of pay deferred, then 50% up to the next 5% of pay deferred
- Allows a 2-year vesting schedule: 0% - year 1 and 100%- year 2
- Requires automatic enrollment of 3% or more and auto increase each year

If your company offers a safe harbor plan, you should receive a safe harbor notice each year at least 30 days prior to the beginning of the plan year announcing this benefit. The notice should let you know which of the above safe harbor types your plan has in place. If not, be sure to review your plan's most current Summary Plan Description.

Chapter 3

401(k) Plan Provisions

Let's review some common and unique 401(k) plan design provisions you need to know about

Eligibility Requirements and Entry Dates

Typically, you must be an employee (not a contractor) receiving W-2 income or be a partner of the firm in order to become eligible. There are exceptions, such as being a leased employee. Sole proprietors who receive a 1099 from a company are generally not eligible for that company's 401(k) plan. Instead, sole proprietors may be able to establish their own plan as a "solo" 401(k).

Eligibility in a 401(k) can be as lenient as immediately eligible upon date of hire with no age requirement all the way up to a minimum of age 21 with one year of service and 1000 hours required to become eligible to participate or receive an employer contribution. Some plans may have dual eligibility, meaning that you would have one set of eligibility criteria to make salary deferrals and another set of eligibility criteria to receive an employer contribution, such as a match.

A plan entry date can be added as well. This is the last hurdle to meet before you can participate or receive an employer contribution in the 401(k) plan. This allows an employee to enter the plan once the eligibility criteria has been met. The plan can have immediate entry or monthly, quarterly or semi annual entry dates.

Vesting Schedules

Vesting schedules are often put in place for both discretionary matching and discretionary profit sharing contributions. Vesting means "ownership" of the employer contributions. The longer you work for the company, the more of the employer contribution you will technically "own". Remember that the employer contribution will be in your 401(k) account even if you're not 100% vested, but the vesting schedule will come into play when you leave the company. At that time, the administrator will calculate your vested account balance or the amount you "own". Note that all employee salary deferrals are always required to be 100% immediately vested.

Vesting schedules are typically calculated starting from your date of hire at the company, so if you've been at a company for 5 years and your plan has a 3-year vesting schedule, then you are 100% vested in any discretionary employer contributions because you have been employed for over 3 years meeting the vesting requirements. Here are some examples of common vesting schedules for discretionary matching and profit sharing based on your date of hire:

6-Year Vesting	5-Year Vesting	4-Year Vesting	3-Year Cliff Vesting
0% - year 1	20% - year 1	25% - year 1	0% - year 1
20% - year 2	40% - year 2	50% - year 2	0% - year 2
40% - year 3	60% - year 3	75% - year 3	100% - year 3
60% - year 4	80% - year 4	100% - year 4	
80% -year 5	100% - year 5		
100% - year 6			

Important notes about vesting schedules

Vesting schedules are tethered to a money source, so your plan will likely have more than one vesting schedule. Safe Harbor Basic, Enhanced, and Non-Elective Contributions (NEC) money sources all must be immediately 100% vested. Safe Harbor QACA contributions (see section on Safe Harbor contributions) have a 2-year vesting cliff. Additionally, it is worth reminding you that your own salary deferral contributions, including pre-tax, Roth 401(k), and rollovers into the plan are always 100% immediately vested.

What if you are not 100% vested and leave your employer? Regardless of why you leave, when you request a rollover or distribution, the non-vested portion will be moved into a plan forfeiture account to be used by the plan, and you will receive the remaining *vested* account balance plus or minus any distribution processing fees.

Loans

Loans are often seen as a big no-no in the 401(k) world. Borrowing from your retirement money? Isn't this supposed to be used for retirement? Ideally, yes! However, many plans offer this provision, but be aware of the pros and cons so you can make an informed decision if you do have this option available to you as it can be very tempting to utilize.

Should you need to tap into your retirement savings prior to retirement, there are multiple ways you may be able to access your 401(k) account while you are still working. Loans are an optional feature in 401(k) plans, although not required. If your plan allows for loans, you can borrow from your existing 401(k) account and pay it back via payroll deduction. There may be an option for a general loan or a primary residence loan. Most often; however, you will see the general loan option. It allows you to borrow up to 50% of your vested account balance, up to $50k at one time and repay it within 5 years with a stated rate of interest, which is typically the prime rate plus 1% or 2%. Currently, the prime rate as of this writing is 8.5%. You may have to pay back your loan amount plus 9.5% or more. Oh, those lovely loans!

The good news is that you do not pay taxes on the amount you borrow and the interest you pay goes into your own 401(k) account, so you are not paying it to a bank or a lender like with a bank loan. However, if you are borrowing from your pre-tax dollars, you will be repaying the loan in after-tax dollars to replenish the pre-tax "bucket" that you borrowed from. That means you paid taxes on the loan repayment AND will pay taxes again when you withdraw it later.

If you leave the company before paying off the loan, typically you have 60-90 days to pay the remaining balance in full. If you do not repay it, you will receive a 1099-R tax form for the outstanding balance and it will be treated as an early withdrawal, which may be subject to a 10% early withdrawal penalty plus ordinary income taxes. If loans are available in your 401(k), it is a wise idea to resort to other money sources outside of the plan before tapping into your retirement account.

Hardship Withdrawals

Hardship Withdrawals are commonly available in most 401(k) plans, but not required. If your plan allows for hardship withdrawals, you may only take out money from your 401(k) account for specific "hardship" purposes that are specifically defined by the IRS. Be sure to review the hardship withdrawal provisions in the Summary Plan Description (SPD) provided by your employer. The most common hardship reasons are:

1. To use for a downpayment on your primary residence

2. To pay for unreimbursed medical expenses for you or your dependents

3. To pay for funeral expenses

4. To pay for post-secondary education expenses for you or your dependents

5. To use for disaster relief repairs to your home

Keep in mind that with a hardship withdrawal, you can only take out the amount that you need for the expense and your human resources contact may ask you for documentation of the expense for auditing purposes. If you are under age 59 ½ when you request the hardship, you will pay an early withdrawal penalty of 10% in addition to ordinary income taxes (federal taxes and state depending on where you reside) on the hardship withdrawal amount.

Additionally, a hardship withdrawal is different than a 401(k) loan because you do not repay the amount like you would with a loan. In this case, you are simply taking out the amount you need as long as the amount is available to you in your account. Some 401(k) plans that allow you to take a loan will require you to take a loan before you can take a hardship withdrawal.

In-Service Withdrawals and Disability

You may also be able to access your 401(k) account once you reach age 59 ½ even if you are still working. Some plans allow you to take in-service withdrawals. Beginning at age 59 ½, the 10% early withdrawal penalty disappears. This penalty is also waived if you become permanently disabled as defined by the IRS. However, you will pay ordinary income taxes for any pre-tax salary deferrals as well as any employer contributions in your account.

End of Employment or Retirement

When you end employment or are happily ready to retire at the company sponsoring the 401(k) plan, you qualify to access your 40l(k) savings. Most plans allow these distribution options:

1. Rollover your 401(k) into another qualified plan, such as a 401(k) or ERISA 403(b) with your new employer

2. Rollover into an Individual Retirement Account (IRA)

3. Cash out the 40l(k) or a portion of the balance

4. Keep the 401(k) in the prior employer's plan

Each option will depend on many factors. The rollover option will avoid any taxes and penalties as long as the 401(k) is deposited into another qualified plan or an IRA. You may incur a one-time distribution fee, but you will continue the tax deferred benefit. The cash out option can be done at any age once you terminate employment, regardless of the reason. However, this option will incur ordinary income taxes (think state and federal depending on where you live) and an early withdrawal penalty of 10% if you are under the age of 59 ½.

Keeping the 401(k) in your prior employer's plan may only be an option if your vested account balance is above a certain amount, such as $5k or $7k or more, but going this route may result in participant expenses applying to your account directly. Furthermore, if the company changes providers or plans, your 401(k) will go right along with it and can make it a challenge to track down your 401(k) later down the road. Most financial professionals will agree that it is best to rollover the 401(k) into your new employer's retirement plan, if allowed, or into an IRA, to continue the tax-deferred benefit and compounding interest.

When you terminate employment, you may be able to cash out some of your balance and rollover the rest, if you must access your 401(k) prior to retirement. Remember, any amount you cash out will be subject to ordinary income taxes and likely an early withdrawal penalty of 10% if you are under the age of 59 ½.

Chapter 4

Basic Investment Concepts

It's time to put your 401(k) to work!

**Let's look at basic investment concepts
to help you reach your goals**

Investing In Your 401(k)

Now that you've learned about how to put money into the 401(k) plan and when to take it out of the plan, let's talk about what to do with the money while it's in the plan! One of the main purposes of having a 401(k) is for the opportunity to invest your money to potentially grow your account beyond the inflation rate.

What is the inflation rate and why is it so important to think about? Inflation eats away at the value of your dollar over time. For example, the average cost of a dozen eggs in 1980 was $.84. Today, the national average is about $4.80 depending on where you shop. Think about the cost of so many items in 1980: milk, gas, cars, homes, clothes, plane or train tickets. Compare that to the costs in 1990, 2000, and today. Everything has gone up! This trend will very likely continue to go up.

If you stuff your hard-earned money under the mattress where it has no opportunity to be invested, then by the time you take it out from under your mattress to spend, the actual value of each dollar will be worth much less. This means your $100,000 is now only worth say $75,000, resulting in less buying power for you.

We know that historically inflation rates have continued to increase. In fact, in 2021 and 2022, the inflation rate sky-rocketed to a whopping 7% and 6.5% respectively! That is the exact reason to invest your 401(k) assets so that you have the opportunity to earn money through interest and dividends to stay on top of inflation and more. A prudent rule of thumb when investing in a 401(k) is to target an 8% annual rate of return for the life of your 401(k) plan. This will ideally allow you to stay above the inflation rate to keep the value of your dollar strong when you are ready to retire. Let's check out the U.S. inflation rates.

Annual U.S. Inflation Rates 2013 – 2023

Below is a bar graph showing the U.S. annual inflation rates from 2013-2023. These rates are derived from the Consumer Price Index (CPI), which calculates inflation rates for things like energy, food, and other US consumer goods. The inflation rates can be found on the U.S. Department of Labor website and are calculated monthly by the Bureau of Labor Statistics (BLS).

You can also check out this handy inflation calculator for more information on how inflation effects the value of your dollar over time:

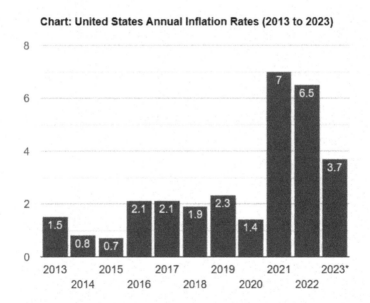

Chart: United States Annual Inflation Rates (2013 to 2023)

https://www.usinflationcalculator.com

These inflation rates are calculated in percentages using the Consumer Price Index, which is published monthly by the Bureau of Labor Statistics (BLS) of the U.S. Department of Labor. CPI Home : U.S. Bureau of Labor Statistics (bls.gov)

Investing *versus* **Vesting**

The idea behind this section is not to get too deep in the weeds and overwhelm you with lots and lots of investment jargon. Instead, the goal is to provide education on basic investment knowledge so that you will feel more comfortable managing your 401(k) account and understand the terminology the next time you're at a dinner party talking about investments. Knowledge is power!

In my 23 years of working in the financial services industry, I have repeatedly heard individuals incorrectly use the terms *investing* and *vesting*. It is time to set the record straight so you will not make that same mistake, and you'll have a clear understanding of what these terms mean. They are very different from each other.

When you hear the term *investing*, it means investing your money in the market and investing your money in investment options. It can be synonymous with the word, *risk*. When you invest your money in the market, you are taking on risk. A 401(k) plan rarely offers an investment option with FDIC insurance, including money market and stable value funds, so if you're wondering if your 401(k) is FDIC insured, the answer is no. However, you have lots of opportunity to grow your money beyond your contributions, which is the tradeoff with investing. There is a risk and reward correlation with investing in a 401(k) plan, which we'll review soon.

When you hear the word *vesting* on the other hand, this is pertaining to a vesting schedule as we learned earlier in Chapter 3 regarding how long you need to work for the company to become fully vested in the employer contributions. Now that we've set the record straight on the difference between the terms investing versus vesting, we'll continue to focus on *investing*.

Basic Investment Concepts

Most 401(k) plans are participant-directed, meaning the employee (participant) directs where to invest his or her 401(k) assets. A prudent plan will offer a variety of funds with a mix of actively and passively managed funds, such as index funds as well as a suite of target date funds or risk-based asset allocation funds or something similar.

Additionally, a solid fund lineup will include multiple fund families. The fund lineup is selected by the employer, often with the help of an investment fiduciary or financial advisor. The employer or investment fiduciary selects the core fund lineup for the plan while the participants choose which funds they want to invest in from that lineup. This is called a participant-directed account.

Some plans offer an additional investing method by way of a self-directed brokerage account window. This option can by far be the riskiest of all. As a plan participant with the brokerage option, you can invest in individual stocks, bonds, ETFs, CITs, and other mutual funds separate from the core fund lineup in the plan.

Stocks, Bonds, Mutual Funds, Oh my!

To understand more, we must review some general investment concepts. Stocks, bonds, and mutual funds are the most common asset classes within a 401(k). To piggy-back off the asset classes, asset allocation is a fancy term for spreading your money around amongst multiple asset classes as a prudent investment strategy to maximize returns and mitigate risk. These asset classes have an inverse relationship between risk versus reward. Some are riskier than others, giving way to higher potential returns while others are less risky and more conservative, resulting in lower returns.

Stocks

Let's look at stocks. When you invest in a stock, you are essentially buying a piece of the company offering the stock. For example, if you buy 100 shares of Microsoft stock, you "own" a piece of Microsoft. Stocks have the most risk of the three types of investments but offer the most potential earnings as well.

Higher risk means higher reward, usually. If you've ever heard the old adage, "don't put all of your eggs in one basket", investing one hundred percent of your 401(k) into one stock would be putting all of your eggs in that one basket, resulting in ultra-high risk for your portfolio. Recall the events of the company, Enron. Employees had 100% of their retirement savings in Enron stock. When that one stock plummeted, so did the entire portfolio. This alone is an excellent reason to diversify your assets.

Bonds

On the other hand, bonds are like an IOU where you lend money to an institution, and it pays you back along with a stated rate of interest. In general, bonds are considered lower risk compared to stocks. With less risk comes less reward. There are many types of bonds out there, such as municipal bonds, corporate bonds, government bonds, and more.

Mutual Funds

What if there were an investment option that provided some level of diversity? I'm happy to say, there is! Mutual funds are a type of investment that are made up of many, many stocks and/or many, many bonds and other investments. If you open the hood of a mutual fund, you will see a list of underlying stocks or bonds or a combination of both. These stocks and bonds will make up that one mutual fund. This in and of itself provides some level of diversification.

But wait, there's more. Within the mutual fund universe, you have a large variety of asset classes that fall under stocks, bonds, or cash. In this book, we're focusing on the most popular investments in a 401(k), which are mutual funds or other types of funds rather than the individual stocks and bonds, like in a brokerage account.

Sticking to mutual funds, which are what you should hope to see available in your 401(k) plan, there are actively and passively managed funds. Actively managed funds are just as they sound. They are actively managed by individuals or a group of individuals aiming to *beat* a specific market index, such as the Russell 2000 Index. Passively managed funds, also called index funds, are designed to *mirror* a specific market index, such as the S&P 500. There are bond funds, stock funds, balanced funds (made up of both bond and stock funds), target date funds, risk-based funds, stable value funds, and more.

Many stock funds are based on the market capitalization of the companies being invested in, which we'll review later in this chapter.

Here is a short list of common types of investment options offered in a 401(k) plan from most aggressive (higher risk, higher potential earnings) to most conservative (low risk, low potential earnings):

Risk Versus Reward Spectrum
By Category

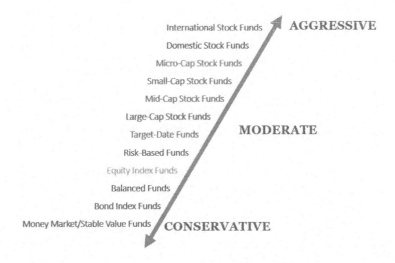

Risk versus Reward spectrum of the most common investment categories in 401(k) plans

International vs. Domestic Stock Funds

Starting at the most aggressive end of the spectrum are international and domestic stock funds. Think of the entire shining, blue globe as international stock funds. They invest in stocks all over the world, both in the US and outside the US. Domestic stock funds; however, invest only in companies within the United States. Either type of stock funds can be made up of companies with a market capitalization of micro, small, mid, large, or even mega-cap.

Market Capitalization of Stocks

Stock funds are often categorized as micro, small, mid, and large cap, or capitalization. Market capitalization means the size of the company the stock fund invests in. More specifically, it is calculated by taking the total shares of outstanding stock at the company and multiply it by the stock price. For example:

Stock Price: $20

# of outstanding shares: 1 million shares

$20 x 1,000,000 = **Market Capitalization of $20,000,000**

Here's a quick look at the types of market capitalization with examples of real companies you've heard of! These numbers and categories will vary depending on the source:

Market Capitalization	Market Value	Examples of Stocks by Market Capitalization	Risk/Reward Spectrum
Micro - Cap	Less than $250M	El Pollo Loco Holdings, Inc. (LOCO) GoHealth, Inc. (GOCO) Unisys Corporation (UIS)	Ultra aggressive/ High Reward potential. Often, newer companies, less stable
Small - Cap	$250M - $2B	AMC Entertainment Holdings, Inc. (AMC) LegalZoom.com, Inc. (LZ) Peloton Interactive, Inc. (PTON)	Aggressive/ High Reward potential, may have huge swings in the market, less stability
Mid - Cap	$2B - $10B	CarMax, Inc. (KMX) U-Haul Holding Company (UHAL) Zillow Group, Inc. (Z)	High to Moderate/ Medium Reward potential, may have moderate swings in the market, more stable
Large – Cap	$10B - $200B	Netflix, Inc. (NFLX) NIKE, Inc. (NKE) Uber Technologies, Inc. (UBER)	Moderate/ Medium Reward potential, stable, long-term companies
Mega-Cap	$200B or more	Amazon.com, Inc. (AMZN) Meta Platforms, Inc. (META) Tesla, Inc. (TSLA)	Moderate/ Medium Reward potential, very stable, long-term companies

Market capitalization is important because it can be a good indicator of the stability of the business, but not always. Companies with a smaller capitalization, or small-cap, are considered high risk with huge potential swings in the market seen in the short-term whereas large-cap and mega-cap companies are perceived as stable companies with longevity and less dramatic swings in the market over time. Remember, when you see market capitalization being described, this is referring to stocks (equities) with a low to very high level of risk.

Target Date Funds

Target Date Funds (TDF) have been around for a long time. These are pre-packaged portfolios based on the year you plan to retire. They are either actively or passively managed and will become more conservative as the target date year approaches. For example, a TDF 2065 portfolio will be invested heavily in stock funds and less in bond or stable value options. You may see an 80/20 split with 80% of the portfolio in stocks funds but only 20% in bond funds or more conservative options. In other words, the portfolio will be actively managed for you in a diversified, aggressive portfolio because the investor retiring in 2065 has about 30 years to ride the ups and downs of the market.

On the reverse, a TDF 2025 portfolio may have a 20/80 split with only 20% in stock funds and 80% in bond funds and stable value options. In both examples, the portfolio allocation becomes more conservative over time as the retirement year approaches. This is a very prudent investment strategy for a long-term retirement savings vehicle like a 401(k) plan.

These funds are also known as a "Fund-of-Funds" because each target date fund is made up of multiple funds within it. TDFs are typically available as a "suite" of Target Date Funds and come in 5 and 10-year increments, such as the American Funds Target Date 2020 Fund or the T. Rowe Price Target Date 2055 Portfolio. It is generally based on the idea that you would retirement around age 65, but if you want to retire at 55, you may select the TDF closest to the year you want to retire. Just keep in mind that the closer the year is to your retirement date, the more conservative the fund will be. This would result in lower risk, but also a lower return than you may be striving for with an early retirement.

Here is an example of the stock versus bond asset allocation for a Target Date Suite in 10-year increments. First, notice the red pie representing the percentage allocated to stocks. See how only 20% is allocated to stocks for the TDF 2020 portfolio but on the other extreme, someone in the TDF 2060 portfolio would have around 85% invested in stocks. Bonds are the inverse of stocks, so to balance out the portfolio, more is allocated to bonds, the more conservative option, as you approach the retirement year because you don't have as much time to ride the ups and downs of the market. This is why roughly 80% is allocated to bonds and only 20% in stocks for the TDF 2020 portfolio.

Hypothetical Target Date Funds
Asset Allocation Changes Over Time

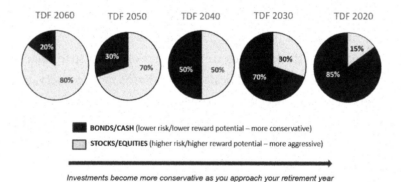

Investments become more conservative as you approach your retirement year

Risk-Based Asset Allocation Funds

Some 401(k) plans offer a suite of risk-based asset allocation funds based on the type of investor you are. You can determine this by completing a risk tolerance questionnaire, which is typically available online in your 401(k) account or you can do a google search or consult with your financial advisor to complete one. You will fall somewhere between a conservative, moderate, or aggressive investor or somewhere in between. These are also pre-packaged portfolios, but rather than being based on the year to retirement, they are based on your risk tolerance level.

The other difference is that the portfolio will always be invested based on a risk-based strategy rather than becoming more conservative as you get close to retirement. That means that if you invest in, say, the Fidelity Moderately Aggressive portfolio, that fund will always invest in options targeting a moderately aggressive investor, resulting in greater risk and reward potential. This may be a good option when you are young and have many years until retirement, but if you leave your money there and 30 years rolls by without proactively changing your investment to a more conservative risk-based portfolio, you may be invested inappropriately. This can put your entire portfolio at a higher risk than necessary. Here is an example of two risk-based portfolios:

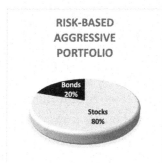

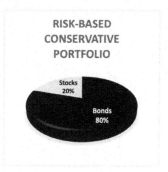

Notice how the aggressive portfolio has 80% in stocks and 20% in bonds. The *conservative* portfolio has only 20% in stocks, but 80% in bonds. Again, risk-based portfolios will always be allocated true to the name of the portfolio, so an *aggressive* risk-based portfolio will always be invested with an *aggressive* approach. On the other hand, a *conservative* risk-based portfolio will always invest with a conservative approach. This is why a participant would need to take action to proactively change which risk-based portfolio is most appropriate for that period of time. For example, if you are an aggressive investor today, a risk-based aggressive portfolio may work for you. However, 10 years from now you may consider yourself a moderate investor, so you'll need to proactively change your portfolio to a moderate risk-based portfolio.

To re-cap, risk-based portfolios stay true to their intended risk tolerance category for the underlying investments. This requires investors to take some action and proactively change into a more appropriate risk-based portfolio as they get closer to retirement or they decide they are a different type of investor at that point in time. Alternatively, target date funds will proactively move into more conservative options for you as your retirement year approaches without the investor needing to take any action at all. If you are looking for a low maintenance, do-it-for-me option, either of these choices will help to accomplish that.

Balanced Funds

Under the hood of a balanced fund you will find a combination of stocks and bonds. These are also referred to as "hybrid" funds. These funds are often allocated into stocks and bonds with moderate to low risk.

Balanced funds, target date funds, and risk-based asset allocation funds are all common default funds within a 401(k). Any of these options can serve as the Qualified Default Investment Alternative (QDIA). If you receive funds into your 401(k) but haven't made an investment election, your funds will go into the default fund selected for the plan. Older plans may still have a money market fund selected as the default fund, but this option no longer qualifies as a QDIA.

Index Funds

Index Funds are passively managed investments. This simply means the funds are not actively managed by money managers attempting to beat the market. Instead, index funds are structured to mirror a specific index in the market. Here are some of the most popular indices you have most likely seen on the news:

Dow Jones Industrial Average (DJIA)
Made up of 30 large-cap blue-chip stock companies, stable companies with long-term track records of success

NASDAQ
Nasdaq Composite, tracks over 3,000 US stocks, heavily weighted in popular tech giants like Amazon and Microsoft

Russell 2000 Index
Made up of 2,000 US small-cap companies

S&P 500 Index
Standard & Poor's 500 Index – comprised of the top 500 US large-cap companies

These are just four of the most common indices, but there are many out there. You will find bond indices as well. In a 401(k), you may see bond index funds as well as equity or stock index funds and if you look at the fund fact sheets, you will see the corresponding index that is used to measure the performance against. Because index funds are not actively managed, they are considered not quite as risky to the average investor.

Money Market and Stable Value Funds

Lastly, we will review the asset category at the bottom of the risk versus reward spectrum. Money Market funds are often used as temporary "parking spots" for 401(k) contributions. If you put ten thousand dollars into a money market fund, it is designed to give you back ten thousand dollars with very little risk. However, it is not a guaranteed fund, so it does not guarantee you'll receive your principal back, although the risk is very low compared to any other category. Money market funds generally have a fund expense ratio, so it is not a *free* account option. It is not a savings account and it is not FDIC insured. It is a low risk investment option that invests in short-term debt securities that are *liquid* (easily turned into cash). They are designed to maintain your original investment called *capital preservation.*

Stable Value Funds are also very low risk investments. When compared to Money Market Funds, they tend to provide slightly higher returns and aim to fight against the effects of inflation by investing in longer term debt securities with a different approach. If your employer changes 401(k) providers and you have money invested in the stable value fund, you are at risk of having to keep a portion of your money in that fund for up to 12 months due to what is called a "12-month Put". This is a provision on a plan level where plan sponsors of a 401(k) must give a 12-month termination notice to their 401(k) provider when they are switching to another 401(k) provider. For example, if your plan moves from John Hancock to Fidelity, you may have to keep your stable value assets at John Hancock for up to 12 months even though the rest of your assets will be at Fidelity.

The purpose of the 12-month Put provision is to protect other investors remaining in the stable value fund from huge market losses. However, one way a participant can avoid this restriction is to transfer out of the stable value fund before the blackout period. This is the period of time when you will be unable to move any money in the plan as the providers prepare to transfer the entire plan. You will receive a blackout notice with specific dates for when it will start and end. Transfer out of the stable value fund *before* the start of the blackout period into other non-competing funds, such as a balanced fund, and the 12-month Put should not apply. There may be exceptions depending on the contract, but that is often how this situation is remedied for many plans.

Chapter 5

FAQs and Key Terms

Let's wrap up with FAQs and key terms to remember

SUMMARY

When it comes to a 401(k) plan, you have a lot to think about. Plan limits, contribution types, tax benefits, investment options, years to retirement. It can be daunting. The good news is that you don't have to be a 401(k) expert or a big shot investment guru to succeed at saving for retirement. Whether you are a do-it-for-me investor or a savvy investor looking to choose your own investment options within your plan, this book helps you make prudent investment decisions and guides you in the right direction towards a retirement where you can live in your golden years both comfortably and with dignity. The best thing you can do for yourself is to start saving now!

Thank you for reading this book!

FAQs

1. **Is my 401(k) protected from creditors?** Yes, your 401(k) account is generally protected from creditors as part of an ERISA plan as an employee. However, in the event of a divorce, your spouse may present a court-order for a portion of your 401(k) called a QDRO. See number 3 below.

2. **Do I have to select my spouse as my beneficiary?** No, but by law, your spouse is automatically entitled as the primary beneficiary unless you have your spouse sign a waiver. Be sure to select a beneficiary who is not a minor or you may need to establish a trust. Refer to your state's regulations for minors.

3. **If I get divorced, can my spouse access my 401(k)?** In the event of a divorce, a Qualified Domestic Relations Order (QDRO) is a court-ordered document that may allow your spouse to a portion of your 401(k).

4. **Can I rollover another 401(k) or IRA into my current employer's 401(k)?** Most likely yes. Refer to your Summary Plan Description (SPD) for which types of prior plans may be rolled over.

5. **Do rollover assets count towards the IRS contribution limits?** No they do not.

6. **Can I take my money out at any time?** No, but remember this is an account for retirement rather than a savings account. Refer to the withdrawal section in Chapter 2. You must meet one of the qualifying events, such as termination of employment, disability, hardship withdrawal, take out a loan, etc.

7. **Can I contribute to the pre-tax 401(k) and Roth 401(k) at the same time?** Yes! If your plan offers the Roth 401(k) provision, you can contribute to both the pre-tax and Roth 401(k) money sources up to the maximum IRS limit, $23,000 for 2024.

8. **Can I contribute to more than one 401(k) plan at a time if I have more than one job?** Yes. However, you can contribute a maximum of $23,000 for 2024 between all plans, not for each one. You would need to monitor your contributions at each company to ensure you do not exceed that amount.

Common Terms To Know

Asset Allocation -   Diversifying your portfolio by investing in multiple asset categories, such as international stock funds, large-cap stock funds, small-cap stocks funds, and bond funds.

Compounding Interest -   Account values grow over time with reinvested earnings and interest on top of 401(k) contributions.

Diversification -   Spreading your money between multiple investments to optimize your overall 401(k) portfolio so that when one investment is down and another is up, it will help to reduce risk

Dollar Cost Averaging -   Contributing to a 401(k) at regular intervals, such as every two weeks, regardless of the ups and downs of the market. One week the cost of a share may be up, another week the cost may be down. Over time, dollar cost averaging results in a lower cost per share.

Risk Tolerance -   This describes how much risk an investor is willing to take in order to receive the desired return. Examples of risk tolerance levels are conservative, moderate, and aggressive or somewhere in between.

Roth 401(k) -   This is a contribution type within the 401(k). An after-tax money source available in some plans. The contributions are post-tax while the earnings are tax-free if held for at least five years prior to age 59 ½.

Rule of 72 - How long will it take your money to double? Take 72 divided by the annual rate of return.
Ex: 72 divided by 8%=9 years
Ex: 72 divided by 2%=36 years

Summary Plan Description (SPD) - A document that each participant receives describing the specific plan provisions available in the 401(k), such as eligibility, matching, profit sharing, vesting, and more.

References

Retirement Topics – Hardship Distributions, Internal Revenue Service, *accessed December 2023.* https://www.irs.gov/retirement-plans/plan-participant-employee/ retirement-topics-hardship-distributions

How Much Salary Can You Defer if You're Eligible for More than One Retirement Plan? Internal Revenue Service, *accessed December 2023* https://www.irs.gov/retirement-plans/how-much-salary-can-you-defer-if-youre-eligible-for-more-than-one-retirement-plan

CPI Tables from the Bureau of Labor Statistics, *accessed December 2023* https://www.bls.gov/cpi/tables/

Retirement Topics – 401(k) and Profit-Sharing Plan Contribution Limits, Internal Revenue Service, *accessed December 2023.* https://www.irs.gov/retirement-plans/plan-participant-employee/ retirement-topics-401k-and-profit-sharing-plan-contribution-limits

Market Capitalization Explained, FINRA, *accessed December 2023.* https://www.finra.org/investors/insights/market-cap

What You Should Know About Your Retirement Plan. Employee Benefits Security Administration, Department of Labor, *accessed December 2023.* https://www.dol.gov/agencies/ebsa/about-ebsa/our-activities/ resource-center/publications/what-you-should-know-about-your-retirement-plan

Stock research by market capitalization, Stock Analysis, *accessed December 2023.*
https://stockanalysis.com/